Instant Memories™

Babies

READY-TO-USE SCRAPBOOK PAGES

Sandra Evertson

Sterling Publishing Co., Inc. New York
A Sterling/Chapelle Book

Author: Sandra Evertson

Paris Flea Market Designs.com
Shabbytiques.com (for Sandra Evertson originals)
Sherrill and Co.com (artist contact management)

If you have any questions or comments, please contact:
Chapelle, Ltd., Inc., P.O. Box 9252, Ogden, UT 84409
(801) 621-2777 • (801) 621-2788 Fax
e-mail: chapelle@chapelleltd.com
Web site: www.chapelleltd.com

Instant Memories is a trademark of Sterling Publishing Co., Inc.

PC Configuration: Windows 98 or later with 128 MB Ram or greater. At least 100 MB of free hard disk space. Dual speed or faster CD-ROM drive, and a 24-bit color monitor.

Macintosh Configuration: Mac OS 9 or later with 128 MB Ram or greater. At least 100 MB of free hard disk space. Dual speed or faster CD-ROM drive, and a 24-bit color monitor.

10 9 8 7 6 5 4 3 2 1

Published by Sterling Publishing Co., Inc.
387 Park Avenue South, New York, NY 10016
© 2005 by Sterling Publishing Co., Inc.
Distributed in Canada by Sterling Publishing
c/o Canadian Manda Group, 165 Dufferin Street
Toronto, Ontario, Canada M6K 3H6
Distributed in Australia by Capricorn Link (Australia) Pty. Ltd.
P. O. Box 704, Windsor, NSW 2756, Australia
Printed and Bound in China
All Rights Reserved

Sterling ISBN 1-4027-2379-2

For information about custom editions, special sales, premium and corporate purchases, please contact Sterling Special Sales Department at 800-805-5489 or specialsales@sterlingpub.com.

Introduction

Scrapbooking is a wonderful way to document special day-to-day events, holidays, celebrations, and family history. However, not everyone has the time or the money to do what it takes to create show-stopping scrapbook pages. That's where the *Instant Memories™ Ready-to-Use Scrapbook Page* series comes in. The top designers in the field have done all the work for you—simply add your favorite photos to their layouts and you're done! Or add a few embellishments, such as a charm or ribbon, and you have a unique personalized page in minutes. You can tear the pages directly from the book, photocopy them to use time and again, or print them from the enclosed CD.

As an added bonus in the *Instant Memories* series, we have included hundreds of rare, vintage images on the enclosed CD-rom. From Victorian postcards to hand-painted beautiful borders and frames, it would take years to acquire a collection like this. However, with this easy-to-use resource, you'll have them all right here, right now, to use for any computer project over and again. Each image has been reproduced to the highest quality standard for photocopying and scanning and can be reduced or enlarged to suit your needs.

Perfect for paper crafting, scrapbooking, and fabric transfers, *Instant Memories* books will inspire you to explore new avenues of creativity. We've included a sampling of ideas to get you started, but the best part is using your imagination to create your own projects. Be sure to look for other books in this series as we continue to search the markets for wonderful vintage images.

How to Use This Book

General Instructions:

The art pages in this book are printed on one side only, making it easy to simply tear out the pages and use as is, or if you choose you can cut out individual images to use on our own pages and projects. However, you'll probably want to use them again, so the enclosed CD-Rom contains all of the images individually as well as in the page layout form. The images are large enough to use at 12" x 12". The CDs can be used with both PC and Mac formats. Just pop in the disk. On a PC, the file will immediately open to the Home page, which will walk you through how to view and print the images. For Macintosh users, you will simply double-click on the icon to open. The images may also be incorporated into your computer projects using simple imaging software that you can purchase specifically for this purpose—a perfect choice for digital scrapbooking.

The reference numbers printed on the back of each image in the book are the same ones used on the CD, which will allow you to easily find the image you are looking for. The numbering consists of the book abbreviation, the page number, the image number, and the file format. The first file number (located next to the page number) is for the entire page. For example, BAB01-01.jpg would be the entire image for page 1 of Babies. The second file number is for the top-right image. The numbers continue in a counterclockwise fashion.

Once you have resized your images, added text, created a scrapbook page, etc., you are ready to print them. Printing on cream or white cardstock, particularly a textured variety, creates a more authentic look. You won't be able to tell that it's a reproduction! If you don't have access to a computer or printer, that's ok. Most photocopy centers can resize and print your images for a nominal fee, or they have do-it-yourself machines that are easy to use.

Ideas for Using the Images:

Scrapbooking: These images are perfect for both heritage and modern scrapbook pages. Simply use the image as a frame, accent piece, or border. For those of you with limited time, the page layouts in this book have been created so that you can use them as they are. Simply print out or photocopy the desired page, attach a photograph into one of the boxes, add your own journaling, and you have a beautiful designer scrapbook page in minutes. Be sure to print your images onto acid-free cardstock so the pages will last a lifetime.

Cards: Some computer programs allow images to be inserted into a card template, simplifying cardmaking. If this is not an option, simply use the images as accent pieces on the front or inside of the card. Use a bone folder to score the card's fold to create a more professional look.

Decoupage/Collage Projects: For decoupage or collage projects, photocopy or print the image onto a thinner paper such as copier paper. Thin paper adheres to projects more effectively. Decoupage medium glues and seals the project, creating a gloss or matte finish when dry, thus protecting the image. Vintage images are beautiful when decoupaged to cigar boxes, glass plates, and even wooden plaques. The possibilities are endless.

Fabric Arts: Vintage images can be used in just about any fabric craft imaginable: wall hangings, quilts, bags, or baby bibs. Either transfer the image onto the fabric by using a special iron-on paper, or by printing the image directly onto the fabric, using a temporary iron-on stabilizer that stabilizes the fabric to feed through a printer. These items are available at most craft and sewing stores. If the item will be washed, it is better to print directly on the fabric. For either method, follow the instructions on the package.

Wood Transfers: It is now possible to print images on wood. Use this exciting technique to create vintage plaques, clocks, frames, and more. A simple, inexpensive transfer tool is available at most large craft or home improvement stores, or online from various manufacturers. You simply place the photocopy of the image you want, face down, onto the surface and use the tool to transfer the image onto the wood. This process requires a copy from a laser printer, which means you will probably have to get your copies made at a copy center. Refer to manufacturer's instructions for additional details. There are other transfer products available that can be used with wood. Choose the one that is easiest for you.

Gallery of Ideas

These Babies images can be used in a variety of projects;
cards, scrapbook pages, and decoupage projects to name a
few. The images can be used as they are shown in the layout, or you can copy and clip out individual images, or
even portions or multitudes of images. The following
pages contain a collection of ideas to inspire you to use
your imagination and create one-of-a-kind treasures.

Idea 1

Circular cutouts of old-time
poetry and thoughts journaled
on a vintage postcard can add
a classic touch to any baby
photo—new or old.

art page 36

Idea 2 A touch of satin ribbon lends further softness when capturing memories of younger days.

art page 37

Idea 3 **I**nclude baby photos on a page for a newlywed couple celebrating the merging of their separate lives into one.

art page 45

art page 44

Idea 4 Hand-striped paper and a flowered border make the perfect setting for sugar-and-spice and everything-nice little girls.

Idea 5 Personalize a child's baby page by adding their name and journaling in a fun memory that they might enjoy a few years down the road.

art page 21

Idea 6 Photocopy the baby's birth certificate or footprint and place alongside a newborn hospital photo.

art page 20

Idea 7 $\mathcal{T}$ransferring vintage images to cloth and accenting a handmade quilt will help to create a gift that will be treasured for years.

Idea 8

Create a fun and charming place to hang special keepsake outfits by decoupaging a wooden hanger.

Idea 10

A tiny little pot for a wonderful new arrival. A great way to decorate baby's room or announce to the world that junior is here.

Idea 9

Blocks collaged with storybook pages can be used as bookends, or mount photos to every side for cube-frames that show off baby from any angle.

Idea 11   Try layering small photos over the back side of the decoupaged circles and stars, so baby can see familiar faces anytime.

Idea 12

Decoupage the sleepy moon art onto plywood, balsa wood, or foam core. Repeat using other decorative papers cut into stars and circles. Bend a heavy-gauge copper wire into shape for the hanging rod, then attach thinner wire from which to dangle the other elements.

BAB01-02

BAB01-03

BAB01-04

| 1 | BAB01-01 |

BAB02-02

BAB02-03   BAB02-04

BAB02-01 — 2

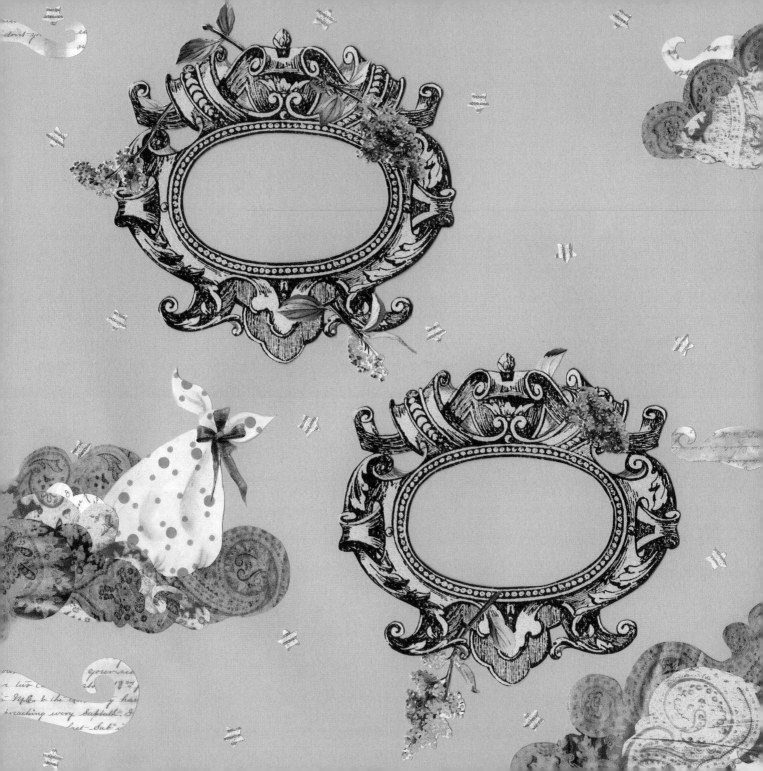

BAB03-02

BAB03-03

3 — BAB03-01

BAB04-04

BAB04-03

BAB04-05

BAB04-02

BAB04-06

BAB04-07

| BAB04-01 | 4 |

Her face is _____ May-time,
Her _____ _____ _____'s;
The su_____ _____ words.

Each _____ the brighter,
As _____ the sun;
And she _____ and cherished
And loved by every one.

By old folk _____
By l_____
Who is _____ _____ _____?

BAB05-02

BAB05-03

5 — BAB05-01

BAB06-04

BAB06-03

BAB06-02

BAB06-08

BAB06-07

BAB06-06

BAB06-05

BAB06-01 — 6

FIRST JOURNEYS

1. Two villagers sat by a tree in Nursery Village. Three villagers were under another tree. How many villagers were there in all?
2. Three villagers and one villager were in front of a row of trees. In all there were —— villagers.
3. Three villagers were in the Nursery Flier and three more waited for a ride. How many in all?
4. Three big villagers and eight little villagers were talking on the corner. How many in all?
5. Three village dogs were chasing ten village cats. How many village animals were running?
6. Three village horses and twenty-one village cows were in a pasture. How many animals in all?
7. A street in Nursery Village had 3 green houses and 15 red houses. How many houses in all?

IN NUMBERLAND

1. Little Bo Peep has a dozen sheep. Three of them are running away. The rest are following her. How many sheep are following Bo Peep?
2. If 3 more sheep run away, how many sheep will Little Bo Peep have left?
3. If Bo Peep has 11 sheep and sells 3, how many will she then ——
4. Bo Peep's ——

BAB07-04

BAB07-03

BAB07-02

BAB07-07

BAB07-05

BAB07-06

7 — BAB07-01

BAB08-04

BAB08-03   BAB08-02

BAB08-05

BAB08-12   BAB08-11

BAB08-10

BAB08-06   BAB08-07   BAB08-08   BAB08-09

BAB08-01   **8**

120

NEW YORK TOY STORE

8c 7c 1c 2c 6c 9c 4c 3c 10c 5c 9c

6¢

Mother gave Edith and John mo...
1. How many horses can they buy ...
2. How many Noah's Arks will 18 cents bu...
...lls can they buy for 2 cents...
...an they buy for 14 cents?
...w for 12 cents?

_____ cents.

...st _____ cents.

blue figures.
6, 7, 8, 9, 10.
e picture by twos.
s. Count them by 2's.
w count them by twos.
count.
black figures.
6, 7, 8, 9, 10.
9 children by 2's.

BAB09-03   BAB09-02

                            BAB09-08

BAB09-04   BAB09-07

BAB09-05   BAB09-06

9 — BAB09-01

BAB10-02

BAB10-03   BAB10-04

Love's Symbols

BAB11-03

BAB11-02

BAB11-04

11 ─ BAB11-01

BAB12-01

To My Valentine.

good wish
ds
oy a
each

BABY'S BIRTHDAY

BAB13-03   BAB13-02

BAB13-04

BAB13-05

                                           BAB13-08

                                  BAB13-07
13 —[BAB13-01]   BAB13-06

BAB14-03   BAB14-02

BAB14-08

BAB14-04

BAB14-07

BAB14-05   BAB14-06

| BAB14-01 | 14 |

BAB15-02

BAB15-03

BAB15-08

BAB15-04

BAB15-07

BAB15-06

BAB15-05

15 — BAB15-01

BAB16-04

BAB16-03

BAB16-02

BAB16-08

BAB16-05

BAB16-06

BAB16-07

BAB16-01 16

BAB17-02

BAB17-03

BAB17-04

BAB17-05

BAB17-08

BAB17-06

BAB17-07

17 — BAB17-01

BAB18-02

BAB18-04   BAB18-03

BAB18-06

BAB18-05

BAB18-01   **18**

BAB19-03   BAB19-02

                                                                              BAB19-04

19 — BAB19-01

BAB20-03

BAB20-02

BAB20-04   BAB20-12   BAB20-11   BAB20-10

BAB20-09

BAB20-08

BAB20-05   BAB20-06   BAB20-07

| BAB20-01 | 20 |

BIRTH RECORD

YEAR — MONTH

DAY — HOUR

NAME

WEIGHT

Your
Photo
here

Baby

♥ GREETINGS ♥

BAB21-04

BAB21-03   BAB21-02

                                      BAB21-08

                                      BAB21-07

BAB21-05
                                      BAB21-06

21 — BAB21-01

BAB22-03

BAB22-02

BAB22-04

BAB22-05

BAB22-06

BAB22-01 — 22

BAB23-01

BAB24-03   BAB24-02

BAB24-04   BAB24-05

BAB25-03   BAB25-02

BAB25-04   BAB25-05

BAB25-01

BAB26-04

BAB26-03

BAB26-02

BAB26-08

BAB26-05

BAB26-06

BAB26-07

PAPER TOY SHOP

TABLE 1 PIN
CHAIR 2 PINS
BED 3 PINS
BARN 4 PINS
PINWHEEL
5 PINS

DOLL 6 PINS
CORNUCOPIA
7 PINS
BASKET 8 PINS
PICTURE
FRAME 9 PINS
HOUSE 10 PINS

BAB27-03   BAB27-02

BAB27-04

BAB27-05

BAB27-06   BAB27-07

27 — BAB27-01

BAB28-01

Baby's

First Picture

BAB29-02

BAB29-03

BAB30-03   BAB30-02

BAB30-04

BAB30-05

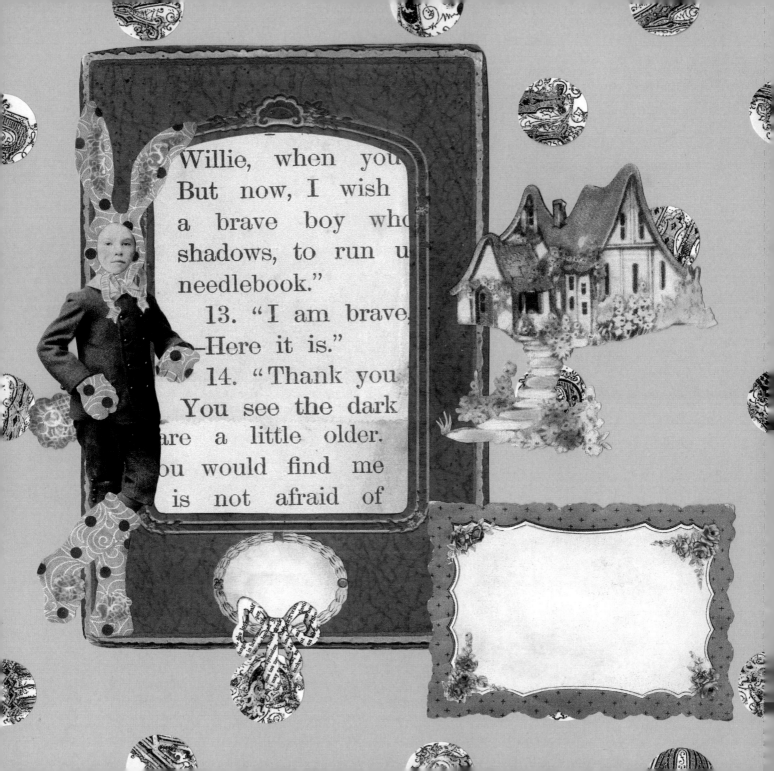

Willie, when you
But now, I wish
a brave boy who
shadows, to run u
needlebook."

13. "I am brave,
—Here it is."

14. "Thank you
You see the dark
are a little older.
ou would find me
is not afraid of

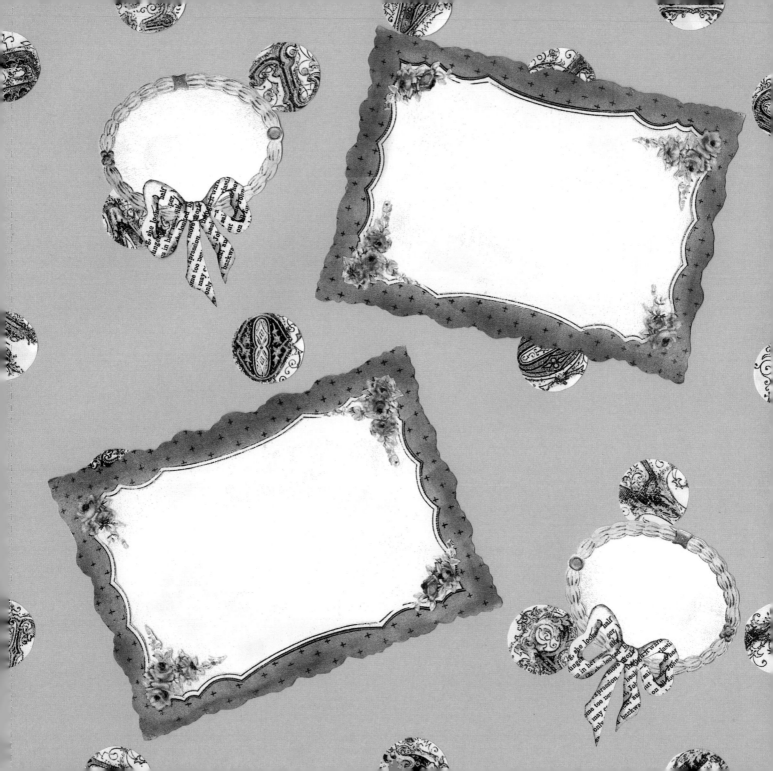

BAB31-03   BAB31-02

BAB31-04

BAB31-05

—| BAB31-01 |

BAB32-03

BAB32-02

BAB32-04

BAB32-05

BAB32-01 32

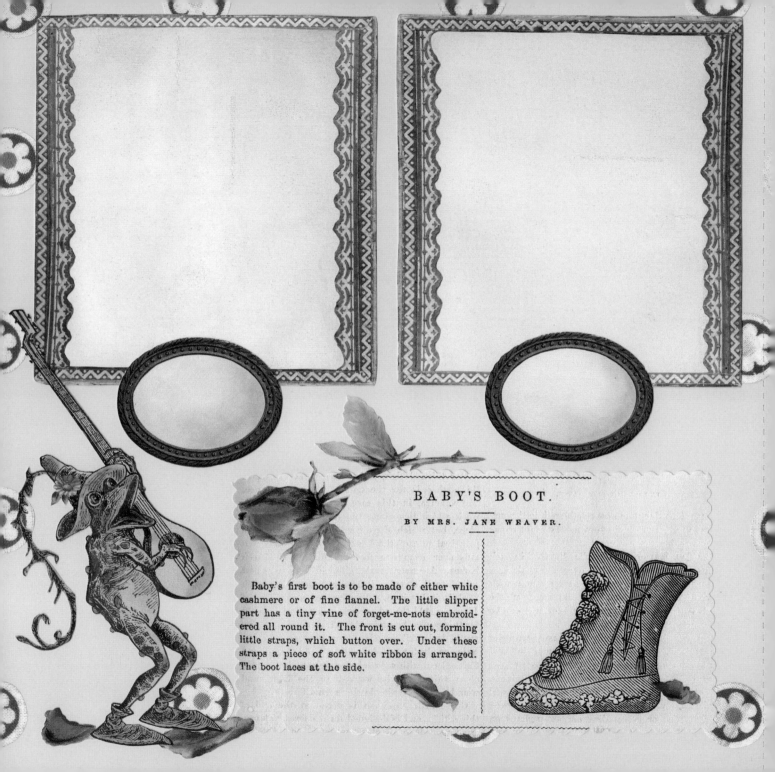

BABY'S BOOT.

BY MRS. JANE WEAVER.

Baby's first boot is to be made of either white cashmere or of fine flannel. The little slipper part has a tiny vine of forget-me-nots embroidered all round it. The front is cut out, forming little straps, which button over. Under these straps a piece of soft white ribbon is arranged. The boot laces at the side.

BAB33-03   BAB33-02

                                                    BAB33-06

BAB33-04

                                                    BAB33-05

33 ─ BAB33-01

BAB34-03

BAB34-02

BAB34-04

BAB34-05

BAB34-08

BAB34-06   BAB34-07

BAB34-09

BAB34-01 | 34

BABY'S
Height and Weight

	HEIGHT	WEIGHT
AT BIRTH		
1 WEEK		
2 WEEKS		
3 "		
4 "		
6 "		
2 MONTHS		
3 "		
6 "		
1 YEAR		
2 YEARS		
3 "		
4 "		

BAB35-03

BAB35-02

BAB35-04

BAB35-09

BAB35-08

BAB35-05

BAB35-06

BAB35-07

35 — BAB35-01

BAB36-03

BAB36-02

BAB36-04

BAB36-05

BAB36-01

36

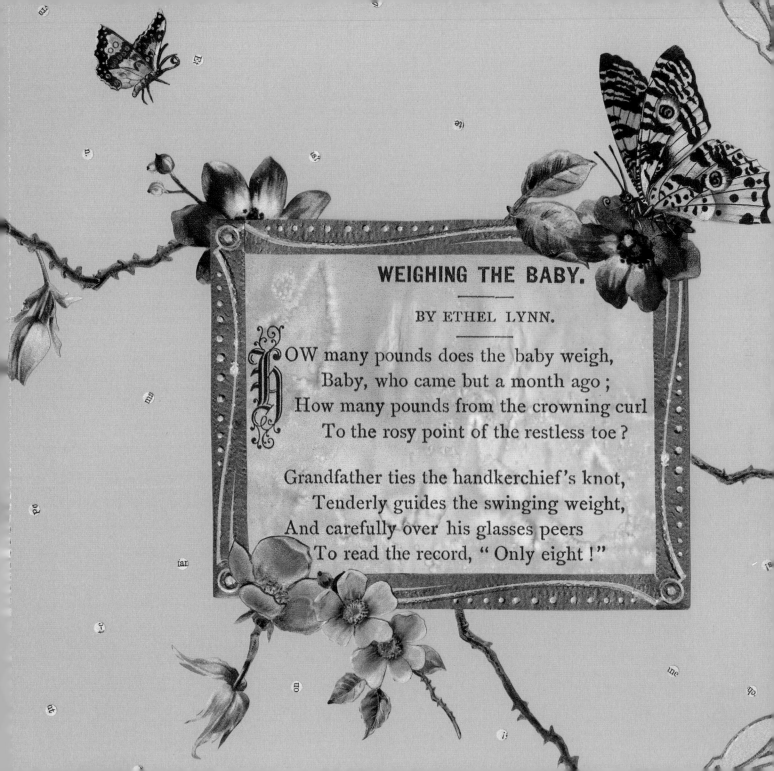

WEIGHING THE BABY.

BY ETHEL LYNN.

HOW many pounds does the baby weigh,
Baby, who came but a month ago;
How many pounds from the crowning curl
To the rosy point of the restless toe?

Grandfather ties the handkerchief's knot,
Tenderly guides the swinging weight,
And carefully over his glasses peers
To read the record, "Only eight!"

BAB39-03   BAB39-02

BAB39-04

                                    BAB39-07   BAB39-06

BAB39-05

— BAB39-01

BAB40-04

BAB40-02

BAB40-03

BAB40-05

BAB40-08

BAB40-06

BAB40-07

| BAB40-01 | 40 |

Just arrived.

MORAVIA, N.Y.

BAB43-04

BAB43-05   BAB43-03   BAB43-02

BAB43-12

BAB43-06   BAB43-11

BAB43-13

BAB43-07   BAB43-08   BAB43-09

43 — | BAB43-01 | BAB43-10

BAB44-04   BAB44-03   BAB44-02

BAB44-05

BAB44-06

BAB44-01   44

k like showir clouds in the distan

rainy season is just commencing

here, it was very dry & dusty when I

came here, I have lots of nice fruit

to eat here, peaches, prunes, raisins, g

kberries, figs, melons &c, dont yo

& I will get fat.

it is very warm

york

ed

de a

same

orlee

it a

like shower clouds in the distan
rainy season is just-commencing
here, it was very dry & dusty when I
me here, I have lots of nice fruit
out here, peaches, prunes, raisins, g
t. Mberries, figs, melons &c, dont yo
d I will get fat.
ir is very warm t

ty three before
hundred ... sal... A. his wife
year before
Edwin ... kno
day of ... he w
came Isaac
persons descri
and they se
the same; and th
need afiant
executed ... hom her
Abm. J.W. Van Vec
Commissioner

BAB45-04   BAB45-03   BAB45-02

BAB45-05   BAB45-08

                              BAB45-06   BAB45-07

45 — BAB45-01

BAB46-02

BAB46-04   BAB46-03

BAB46-05   BAB46-09

BAB46-06   BAB46-08

              BAB46-07   BAB46-01   46

BAB47-03   BAB47-02

BAB47-04

                                                  BAB47-07

BAB47-05   BAB47-06

47 — BAB47-01

BAB48-02

BAB48-06

BAB48-03   BAB48-05

BAB48-04   BAB48-01 **48**

BAB51-04   BAB51-03   BAB51-02

                          BAB51-09

                               BAB51-08

                                         BAB51-07

BAB51-05

                          BAB51-06

51 — BAB51-01

BAB52-02

BAB52-03

BAB52-04

BAB52-07

BAB52-05

BAB52-06

BAB52-01 — **52**

Happy Memories

BAB53-02

BAB53-03

BAB53-08

BAB53-04

BAB53-05   BAB53-06   BAB53-07

53 — BAB53-01

BAB54-02

BAB54-03

BAB54-07

BAB54-04   BAB54-05   BAB54-06

BAB54-01 — 54

BAB55-03

BAB55-02

BAB55-04

BAB55-08

BAB55-05

BAB55-06

BAB55-07

BAB55-01

BAB56-03

BAB56-02

BAB56-04

BAB56-08

BAB56-05

BAB56-07

BAB56-06

BAB56-01 — 56

r, figs, melons &
will get fat.

eather is very warm here,
by an open window, & am
fortable, the nights are quite
that we have a fire in the ev
rning a little while. Uncles
place in their sitting roo
right in the timber, so
of wood to burn,
loud

BAB57-04   BAB57-03   BAB57-02

BAB57-05

BAB57-06

— BAB57-01